I0504390

ABIEGAIL ROSE

Boss Babe by Design

101 Tips to Become a Successful Boss Babe

PUBLICATIONS

First edition

ISBN: 978-0-359-30394-6

This book was professionally typeset on Reedsy.
Find out more at reedsy.com

Contents

Foreword

Hello fellow Boss Babes.

I hope you're ready!

This book is jam-packed with actionable tips. Each created to help you become the successful Boss Babe that you've always desired to be.

Boss Babe by Design is full of content that will make you want to quote it on Instagram and tips that will make you want to put in Work like my favorite bad girl Riri.

Each Boss Babe Design Tip that I'm sharing can be taken a hold of and used right away too. No having to wait a year or exert mass amounts of effort to change the way you do business.

It just takes a little bit of thought, determination, and, of course, Boss Babe Sass!

Toodles,
   Abiegail Rose

1

Introduction

Why strive to become a Boss Babe?

A recent survey found that more than 70% of women want to be some sort of Boss Babe. In today's times, being a Boss Babe, has become synonyms with being a Boss Babe. Many women seek this out for different reasons including pride, purpose, and money. Starting and running your own business on a day to day basis is no easy task, but neither is climbing the corporate ladder and breaking glass ceilings; and they are both truly worth the effort. However, if you're a Boss Babe who's focused on becoming a Boss Babe than this book is for you!

Why consider entrepreneurship?

There are many reasons why you should consider taking that giant step and creating your own business. Here are just a few of them:

Autonomy-

Running your own business allows you to be in charge of your own destiny. It also helps you to avoid getting stuck in the "daily grind" or the "rat race". For many people running their own business lets them have a career that is self-sustaining.

Opportunity-

Being a Boss Babe opens up a whole new world of opportunity for you. You will have the opportunity to do anything that you want in life. This means you can choose to spend your life changing the world for the better, or you can live the type of life you want. Few other career choices can offer this kind of opportunity.

Impact-

Many people who work for other companies truly want to work hard and help that company to succeed, but few are actually able to have such an impact. When you run your own business everything you do will directly impact the company, which can be very rewarding.

Freedom-

This is the answer most people will give if you ask them why they want to become a Boss Babe. For many people the idea of doing what they want and how they want to do is the most compelling reason to take the risk and run their own business. It is true- having freedom in life and career does make a huge difference!

Responsibility-

When you run your own business you have the ability to be responsible to society and operate your business the way that you feel it should be run. This is especially true if you have the desire to help others or the world in general. If you work for someone else you may not be able to improve the world the way you want to, but if you are the boss you can.

Being your Own Boss-

This is another common answer for why many people want to become Boss Babes. If you are your own boss, you can do things your way. You can make your own decisions, take your own risks and decide your own fate.

Time and Family-
Depending on your specific goals in life, becoming a Boss Babe could give you the freedom of time and allow you to spend more of it with your family.

Creating a Legacy-
If the idea of forging a lasting legacy is important to you then a few other careers give you the opportunity to do so like operating your own business.

Accomplishment-
If you have specific goals that you would like to accomplish in your life running your own business could help you to do so.

Control-
For a lot of business owners, the sense of security that comes with the ability to control your own work is a major reason to become a Boss Babe.

What does it take to become a Successful Boss Babe?

There are plenty of benefits of being a Boss Babe, but it is certainly no easy task to start your own business. Successful Boss Babes, that is to say those who are able to accomplish their goals, earn a successful living through their business and enjoy the many benefits of entrepreneurship, all have specific traits. If you are considering taking the leap and following your entrepreneurship dreams, then you will want to understand what these traits are so that you can instill the same traits in yourself. This will help ensure that you are able to achieve your dreams.

Successful Boss Babes:

- Have passion and a lot of it
- Are tenacious
- Can overcome their fear of the unknown
- Have a grand vision
- Believe in themselves
- Are extremely flexible
- Can defy conventional wisdom
- Are willing to take risks in life

If you have these traits, or if you can teach yourself how to develop these traits within yourself, then your likelihood of becoming a successful Boss Babe will increase. In addition to these personality traits, all successful Boss Babes possess a certain amount of skills.

Some Skills That Will Help You to Become a Successful Boss Babe In

Focus- running your own business requires dealing with any number of factors on any given day. Successful business owners are able to pinpoint their focus onto accomplishing specific tasks and goals at specific times.

Resilience- it is a skill to be able to weather the various ups and downs of business without allowing them to destroy your focus. Truly successful Boss Babes are able to continue traveling down the path of success even when the future looks bleak.

Management Skills- a successful company requires the right people and successful business owners need to know how to properly manage these people.

Long-Term Vision- while it is easy to focus on what the company needs to do in the next several days or weeks to be successful, truly exceptional Boss Babes (the ones who see real success in their business ventures) are able to plan years ahead of time.

Sales-womanship- regardless of what type of company you are running, you need to be able to sell your vision to others in order to become successful. Boss Babes need to have great salesmanship skills whether they want to or not.

Self-reliance- this is one of the most important skills any Boss Babe can possess. It is vital for a business owner to trust that they can depend on themselves.

Self-reflection- the ability to pause, reflect and learn is a very valuable skill for the business owner. Boss Babes must be able to learn from their mistakes and reflect upon what they have learned in life.

Learning- the skill of earning knowledge is one that every successful business owner has. It is also a skill that they never stop developing.

To be successful in your entrepreneurial dreams you have to be able to learn from others. The best way to learn the skills of a successful business owner is to study the skills of successful Boss Babes and then to grow those skills in yourself.

2

The Importance of Passion

Passion represents one of the most important aspects of becoming a successful Boss Babe. Without passion your business will turn out to be just another job.

#1- Always choose something you are passionate about!

Without passion, and a lot of it, your business dreams will become lost in the day to day grind of running a business. Take a look at the top ten most successful Boss Babes and you will see that their passion is the number one driving force behind their success. There is no way to escape this fact- you simply must be passionate in order to achieve your goals!

Starting with a Dream

The best way to start a business is to take what you are passionate about and find a way to turn that into a business. You need to start with a dream. If you don't have a passion for your work then you won't have the motivation and energy to keep pushing through obstacles, you won't be willing to take the necessary risks required to succeed and you won't be able to sell your dream to others.

#2- Start with your dreams and grow your business from there.

The unfortunate reality is that once a business reaches the beginning of its third year its chances of surviving drops dramatically. Only about 44% of businesses live to see their fourth year. Without the passion you derive from living your dream you won't have what it takes to survive year after year. This means that you should start your business from the ground up using your dream as a foundation.

Whatever your dream in life may be, you need to find a way to turn that dream into a business. If the foundation of your business is based on something that you are truly passionate about, then it will be much easier to grow that dream into a hugely successful business.

3

Starting Your Dream Business

Once you have determined that you have the necessary traits, skills and passion to become a Boss Babe, the next step will be to start up your dream business.

Getting Started

Getting started with your dream business may be the easiest part of the process, or it may be the hardest. It really depends on your specific situation. Some would-be Boss Babes are raring to get started, while others are bogged down with doubts and procrastination.

#3- Avoid coming up with excuses why you shouldn't start your own business.

Once you have made the important decision that yes you want to become a Boss Babe, skip the excuses and start the process.

#4- Avoid the quicksand that is known as procrastination.

Putting off the process of starting your business for any reason can lead to getting stuck in the mud. Avoid the process of procrastination at all costs.

#5- Do whatever it takes to motivate yourself to get started.

Doubt, fear, worry and a lack of purpose can all end up preventing you from getting your dreams going. Focus on why you want to become a Boss Babe (your passion) and use that to motivate yourself into taking those first few steps. The first couple of steps are the most important ones.

#6- Develop core beliefs.

Now is the time to develop your business's core beliefs. This will help you to create the right kind of company, one that matches your passion and motivates you to always move forward. Your business's core beliefs will be a major building block of it, so make sure that these beliefs are worthy. They will also determine how you proceed to make decisions in the future and which direction the business takes your life.

Making the Shift from Employee to Boss

Running your own business takes leadership. For many new Boss Babes, it can be difficult to make the switch from employee to manager or boss. There are ways that you can prepare yourself for this transition. For people who have built-in leadership skills this transition may be easier, but anyone with the proper drive and motivation can develop leadership skills.

#7- Learn how to listen.

A good boss knows how to listen to their employees and how to recognize good ideas. For a lot of people the concept of being a good listener is hard to contemplate. Learning how to listen probably represents one of the most difficult aspects of turning yourself into a good boss.

#8- Invite creative thinking.

Another trait of a good boss is the ability to invite others to share their ideas with you. You will want to create an atmosphere where your employees will want to share their ideas with you on a regular basis. Great ideas drive businesses forward.

#9- Learn to delegate.

Maintaining control of a company can also mean delegating certain responsibilities to others and good bosses know how to do so success-fully.

#10- Take downtime to reflect.

The responsibility of an employee to learn from their mistakes is not as great as the responsibility of the boss to do so. It is important for any boss to take the appropriate amount of time to stop, think and reflect upon what they have learned. Only through reflection can you truly learn from your mistakes and avoid repeating them in the future.

#11- Expect respect.

Bosses require respect. When making the transition from employee to boss it is important to expect respect from your subordinates.

#12- Earn respect.

While you should be prepared to expect respect from your employees, it is also vital that you be prepared to earn this respect. This is accomplished through honesty, fairness and by giving respect.

Keeping Your Options Open

Starting up a new business requires detailed planning. This means creating various options for how you are going to run your business and then choosing which of these options is the best choice for your business. It is important to keep your options open throughout the start-up process and even through the day to day operations of your business in order to create a resilient and successful business.

#13- Run a lot of forecasts.

It is always a good idea to run through a series of forecasts for your business. Run through the various 'business as usual' forecasts, then add in other scenarios. This will allow you to better forecast your business's future and create different options for dealing with these options. This is especially true for starting up a business.

#14- Gather real market information.

Very few businesses actually end up following their business plans. Plans change all of the time. The best way to create a valuable and functional business plan is to ensure that you create it using real market information.

#15- Understand your market.

Gathering real market information for your business's plan means understanding your business's trends, customers, competitors and various marketing conditions. This kind of information can only be gathered through detailed research.

#16- Plan for failure.

Things will not always go well in your business. Keeping your business options open means understanding this fact and making plans for dealing with failures in advance.

#17- Deal with what you can control and let the rest go.

While you are making plans for dealing with failures along the way make sure that you are focusing on dealing with only the things that you can control. Constantly obsessing over the things, you won't be able to control or attempting to figure out how to control things you simply cannot - gets you nowhere.

#18- Set realistic goals.

Business planning is all about setting up goals and then striving to achieve them. Just make sure that the goals you are setting up for your new business are actually achievable so that you are not setting your business up for failure.

#19- Remember your dreams but plan for goals.

Dreams are what you want to accomplish with your business, but goals are how you will actually go about accomplishing things. Plan for specific goals as a smaller part of accomplishing your dreams.

Choosing a Business Role That Fits Your Personality

Obviously as a Boss Babe your primary business role will be as boss. But this is not the most practical way to plan what you will be doing for the company on a day to day basis. Odds are your company will be more successful if you are able to create a niche for yourself within the company that fits your specific personality.

#20- Determine your strengths and make them your business role.

If you are more confident in one aspect of the business, say selling your ideas to other people, then that is the best way for you to place yourself into the business. Always play to your strengths. Avoid being in charge of selling the company's ideas to others if you are a horrible salesperson.

#21- Avoid doing it all.

Very few successful Boss Babes do it all themselves. Part of being a great business creator is sharing the load in the most effective manner. This will be the reason why you will hire competent and useful people.

Bringing in Professionals

Since you won't be able to do everything required to create a successful business yourself you will have to bring in others. Who you choose to help you operate your company will go a long way towards determining how successful it will be. One of the most important tasks for any Boss Babe to master is the art of hiring the right professionals for the job. You simply cannot afford to lose time, money and results by hiring the wrong people.

#22- View your employees as investments.

Each and every one of your new employees is an investment in your company. On average, the cost of hiring a bad employee for a company is between $25000 and $50,000 a year. Add in training and finding new employees and you can see just how important it is to ensure that you get the proper return on your employee investments.

#23- Hire slow but fire fast.

It is important to take your time and do the right research when it comes to going through the process of hiring an employee. This helps to ensure that you hire the right person for the job. But be ready to get rid of that person as quickly as possible if they aren't working out.

Remember that employees are investments and you want to drop bad investments as soon as possible.

#24- Look for competency.

Valuable employees are competent people. They have the skills, education and experience to get the job done. Figure out what skills you need and hire only professionals who can prove they have the competency to perform those skills.

#25- Check for compatibility.

A good employee can not only do their job properly, but they can also fit into your work environment. You will want to find professionals that are compatible with your business, its goals and its ethics. You also want to hire people who will get along with your employees and customers.

#26- Gauge commitment.

Turning a startup into a successful business requires tons of commitment, from both you and your employees. The right employee is serious about helping the company succeed and has the commitment to see it through. One way to gauge a potential employee's commitment level is to look through their work history.

#27- Choose capable people.

When looking for a new employee you will want to find out if the person is indeed capable of performing their tasks and if they are likely to go beyond their required functions. A capable employee will grow with the company and take on new responsibilities as they become necessary.

#28- Choose people that fit into your company's culture.

Every company has its own distinct culture. This refers to how people communicate with one another, the different expectations they have regarding daily work and the various policies of the company. Employees that don't fit into this culture can often cause problems and diminish efficiency. Therefore, it is always a good idea to hire people that will fit well into the culture of your company.

#29- Plan to compensate appropriately.

It is extremely important for an employee to feel appreciated and appropriately compensated. If you have a good employee, but they feel like they are not being paid what they are worth they will probably under perform at their job. Plan to compensate new employees according to what they are worth and ensure that the new employee is truly satisfied with what you are willing to offer them.

#30- Speak with former co-workers.

Every candidate will provide you with references, but odds are these references are going to provide only positive answers to your questions. You may have to dig a little deeper to discover the real facts about a potential employee. Therefore, it is always a good idea to speak with the candidate's former co-workers, including their past bosses.

4

Managing Others

How well you are able to manage other people will determine whether or not your business is successful. This includes finding the right place for yourself in the company's actions and for hiring employees. Choosing employees who are capable, competent, compatible, committed and who fit into your company's culture will ensure that the day to day aspects of your company are taken care of. Preparing yourself for the challenges of becoming a boss will help make sure that you are able to lead the company to success. But truly successful leaders don't rely purely on their own skills and characteristics. Instead they surround themselves with experts.

Surrounding Yourself with Experts

Experts are people who know more about a specific aspect of a business than you do. It is stupid to try to manage every aspect of the business yourself, as it is to try to claim that you are the most qualified person to do so. The best thing you can do to ensure that the vast majority of the management decisions made are positive and correct is to surround yourself with experts.

#31-Free up your time.

Every decision your business management team makes takes time and effort to create. You need to carefully consider all of the pros and cons and how a particular decision will affect your company and its bottom line. The more you rely on experts to help you with this research the more time you will have to run the other parts of your company.

#32- Choose niche-specific experts.

The purpose of hiring experts is to use the knowledge and skills of other people to accomplish certain tasks better than you could on your own. Therefore, it makes sense to choose experts in very specific niches. For example, one of your managers could be an expert in finances, while another is a marketing genius. This way you don't have to be a master of either of these things to excel in them.

#33- Recognize your own weaknesses.

The best way to hire the best experts is to understand where you need the expertise of other people. This means you must have an understanding of where your knowledge is the weakest.

#34- Choose experts to fulfill your business's overall vision.

If you are able to find niche-specific experts that all buy into the same overall vision for the company then odds are your company will see sustained growth.

Being a Positive Leader

Being a leader is difficult and it requires many traits and skills. The most important of these is a positive attitude. Your mental attitude will determine how you experience every aspect of your life, including how you run your business. It will also have a tremendous influence on how you act as a leader and how well you are able to influence your employees. Even though maintaining a positive attitude on a daily basis can be a tricky thing to do, it is one of the most important aspects of being a good leader and it will have many positive effects on your business.

#35 - Smile a lot.

One of the simplest ways to maintain a positive mental attitude on a daily basis is simply to smile a lot around the office. When you smile it causes other people to smile and generally displays a happy and positive attitude that others will emulate.

#36 - Find good things to say to other people.

People like compliments and the simple act of saying something nice to someone can go a long way towards changing their attitude and their performance. The more you work to find nice things to say about people the easier it will be to come up with things.

#37 - A positive attitude will increase productivity.

Happy workers are productive workers. The happier and more adjusted your employees are the harder they will work and the more productive your company will be.

#38 - You don't need to be unrealistically upbeat.

Maintaining your positive attitude day in and day out can be very difficult, especially when the stresses and strains of everyday life get in the way. Your employees will look to you during the tough times and act the way you do. If you are positive and upbeat they will be too. That being said you don't need to be unrealistically upbeat all of the time, or else you may seem fake. Even in the most trying of times a simple change in perception or recognition of something positive can make a world of difference.

#39- Focus on only the things that you can change.

Again, it doesn't make sense to try to change things that are beyond your control. Focus on altering only the things that are within your power to change and work on how you perceive the things you cannot change.

#40- Give credit where credit is due.

One of the best things that you can do to create a positive working environment is to give credit to your employees when it is due. No one can do it all themselves, so when the company is doing well it is because of the hard work of all of the employees. Giving credit when it is deserved will increase worker morale and encourage them to keep up the good work.

#41- Whenever possible give credit in front of others.

When you do give an employee credit for their hard, try to say positive things to them in front of other employees and even customers. This increases the praise for the employee and portrays a positive attitude for other people to see. It also increases the image that you are indeed a positive leader.

#42- Empower your employees by allowing them to make their own decisions.

You chose to hire your employees because of their various skills and traits. Now is the time to empower them to do their jobs by trusting them to make their own decisions. Believe that they are doing their best to help the company achieve its goals and let them do their job.

#43- Don't second-guess your employee's decisions.

Even if a specific decision turns out to be a wrong one it is never a good idea to second-guess it. No one likes to be second-guessed and it will ruin the trust you have built up with your employees. Instead of constantly scrutinizing your worker's decisions, hear them out. Ask why they made a particular decision under the circumstances and use it as a training opportunity.

#44- Deal with any problems directly and honestly.
The best way to deal with any problems with your employees is to be both direct and honest. You don't need to crush someone's spirits, nor do you have to cushion them with compliments or sugar coat it for them. Direct honesty will get you far more respect and it will help you to more effectively deal with the problem.

#45- Never reprimand an employee in front of others.
Sometimes being a boss means that you have to 'be the bad guy' and reprimand an employee. In addition to being direct and honest with your reprimands, be sure to do them in private. Your employee will respect that and it will help to keep the office attitude positive.

#46- Do nice things for your employees sometimes.
Actions definitely speak louder than words. Every now and then show your workers that you really do appreciate them by doing something nice for them. Just going the extra mile occasionally can make a world of difference.

Understanding Where Conflict Comes From

Whenever you create a group of people and have them work together conflict can happen. Conflict is never a good thing in a professional work environment. It can negatively impact your team's morale and productivity and therefore, your bottom line. One of the best things that you can do as a leader is to understand where such conflict comes from. Once you understand its source you can go about getting rid of it.

#47- Conflict doesn't necessarily have to be a bad thing.

Of course, conflict is bad for business, but it doesn't necessarily have to be the worst thing in the world. Conflict can challenge how people think and create new ideas once it is resolved. Once a conflict between two people is dealt with and overcome, the level of trust and respect between those two people is often increased.

#48- A lack of conflict can represent complacency.

The right amount of workplace conflict means that the company is growing and thinking. A total lack of conflict can mean complacency.

#49- Identify the underlying cause of conflict.

The best way to identify the underlying cause of conflict in your office is to be direct and honest with your employees. Ask them questions. Be prepared to deal with the problem immediately.

#50- Focus on the positive aspects of conflict.

You know that positives like more trust and respect can come out of resolved conflicts, so do your best to focus on these potential positives when dealing with your employees and their problems.

#51- Allow employees to settle their own problems without your intervention.

It is your job to intervene when an employee is mistreating another worker or failing to do their job properly, but you as the boss do not necessarily have to get involved with every employee dispute. In many cases the best course of action is to allow the employees to settle their own problems. Let your workers know that a professional work environment is necessary and while they don't have to be friends, they do have to be professionals.

#52- Get to know your employees in order to understand where conflict comes from.

There is a lot to know about your employees. You should take the time and spend the effort to really get to know your workers, including their strengths and their weaknesses. This will help you to understand the source of most types of conflict that arises around them and will give you the answers to solving the problem.

Listening Skills

Developing your listening skills is one of the most important things you can do to become a good leader and boss. Your employees are a valuable part of your organization and they deserve to be heard. Not only will taking the time to really listen to your workers improve their morale and how they think of you as a boss, but it will also help you to better understand what is really going on at your business. Listening can also open new doors and ideas, which will increase productivity.

#53- Let people finishing talking before you begin to speak.

This is a simple yet effective way to improve your listening skills. Simply let the person finish their point before you intervene. Try not to think about objections to their points while they are talking and don't assume you know what they are going to say before they say it.

#54- Acknowledge the other person's points.

You don't have to agree with their points, but you should at least acknowledge that you understand them. Repeat the person's main concerns in your own words after they have finished speaking in order to acknowledge that you have truly heard and understood them.

#55- Sometimes just listening can be enough.

In some cases, you may not have to take any action to resolve the person's problem. Sometimes simply listening to their problems and acknowledging that you understand, can be enough. Hearing out an employee can often help them feel empowered and significant, which may end up fixing the problem on its own.

#56 - Let your employees know that you are available.

Being a good listener also means making sure that people know that you are accessible. Make sure that your employees know that you are willing to listen to them when necessary and that you are available to do so.

#57 - Remember that your employees are people.

It is always a good idea to remember that your employees are people and that they will have bad days and problems of their own. Of course it is the employee's responsibility to deal with their own personal issues outside of work, but it never hurts to remember that they are indeed humans. Your employees are not just cogs in your business's wheel - they are actually the heart and soul of your company and deserve to be treated as such.

5

Staying Motivated

A positive attitude and a lot of passion are absolutely necessary to run a successful business over the long term. Your passion and dream will be your motivation during this process. However, the daily ups and downs of running a business, along with the occasional misstep, will often diminish your motivation. This can have severe consequences. Without proper and long-lasting motivation, the odds of your business surviving for years to come will be reduced. The good news is that there are plenty of things you can do to help maintain your own motivation and to help motivate your staff.

Positive Thoughts

Again, so much of running your own business comes down to positive thoughts. Staying positive and changing how you think about life can help ensure that you stay motivated during difficult times.

#58- Seek out support.

Being a Boss Babe is difficult work. Sometimes it can help to reach out to others, especially if they are also Boss Babes. Seeking out support from other people who are facing similar challenges can help you retain your motivation and find new innovative ways to solve your problems. Support from others can also help you have a little fun and remember why you wanted to be a Boss Babe in the first place.

#59- Believe in your ability to accomplish your dreams.

However, you go about achieving this, it is important to replenish your belief in yourself on a regular basis. Some people accomplish this by creating a motivation wall, while others have regular meetings with a mentor or life coach. Even just taking a few minutes each day to tell yourself that you have what it takes to succeed can motivate you to keep going.

#60- Get away from work for a while.

Every mind needs a little rest. It is important to get away from your business and your entrepreneurial mindset every now and then, simply to allow your brain to rest and recuperate. This is a great time to engage in a hobby and get some exercise. Exercise is vital to a healthy mind and by taking some time to relax and refresh you will find that you are able to return to work with more motivation.

Learning How to Manage Your Time

Properly managing your time will help you not only to be more productive, but it will also help ensure that you remain motivated. Every successful Boss Babe has good time management skills.

#61- Forget 'clock time'.

Traditional time management wisdom is designed to help you manage your 'clock time', or actual minutes on the clock. This is not really how you spend your day, however. You may want to consider forgetting about 'clock time' and focus on real time. Real-time is how much of your day you spend on each activity, both in work and at home. Real-time is relative.

#62- Choose how much time you want to spend on specific things.

Since real-time is relevant, you have the power to choose how much of your time you spend on specific activities. As a business owner you may not be able to stop interruptions and problems, but you can choose how much time you want to spend dealing with them. Decide how much time you want to spend thinking about things, conversing about things and acting on things, then match your available time appropriately.

Working When You Are Most Productive

Part of learning how to better manage your time means learning to organize your efforts so that you are working when you are likely to be the most productive. This process helps to eliminate wasted time, or when you are working but not being particularly productive.

#63- Record your activities for a week.

To learn how to work when you are the most productive you can start by carrying a schedule book with you and recording all of your thoughts, conversations and actions for a period of one week. This will give you a clear understanding of how much time you spend on each activity, which will allow you to determine which activities are productive and which are less than productive.

#64- Create a schedule for only the most productive activities.

Once you understand which activities are productive and which are wasting your time you can go about ensuring that you only schedule your time around the productive activities. Create blocks of time for yourself for activities that are high-priority and make sure that you determine how much time is appropriate to spend on each activity.

#65- Have discipline.

Once you understand where and when you are spending your time, on both productive and unproductive activities, have enough discipline to appropriately schedule your time.

#66- Plan your day.

Take 30 minutes or so at the beginning of each day to make detailed plans of what you plan to do and what you plan to accomplish. Make sure to plan out at least 50% of your daily time towards your most productive activities. Also plan for interruptions, or times when you will be pulled away from your work. Decide what you want to accomplish before every meeting or telephone call to make each more productive.

#67- Don't be afraid of the 'do not disturb' sign.

There should be a certain part of your day where you really need to get work done and a 'do not disturb' sign can help ensure that you are actually able to get work done.

#68- Watch for distractions.

Your cell phone, social media services and e-mail services are all great ways to stay in touch with employees and customers, but they are also extremely distracting. Plan some time to answer your e-mails, texts and calls, but avoid answering a text or call just because it is coming in. Constantly communicating is a drain of your valuable time. Understand when a text or call is critical to business and when it is not so important.

#69- Remember that not everything will get done.

It is simply impossible to get everything you want to be done. You are never going to get it all done and you will drive yourself crazy if you attempt to do so. Also remember that about 80% of the results you produce are done with about 20% of your time. By learning how to work when you are most productive and by making the most of your productive time you will be able to get what really needs to be done completed.

Tips for Maintaining Motivation

There are other things you can do to make sure that you stay motivated to keep working towards success on a daily basis.

#70- Alter your routine.

Routines often become depressing reminders of the daily grind. By altering your routine, even the slightest bit, you may be able to create a fresh new feeling. This could mean having a meeting outdoors or in a coffee shop. Anything that represents something different from your everyday life can have a very refreshing effect on you and your employees.

#71- Move around.
  This one may sound simple, and that's because it is. But walking or moving around often can help break up the day and keep you motivated. It is also better for your physical and mental health to move around every 30 minutes or so.

#72- Offer incentives for productivity.
  Offering incentives for yourself and your employees in exchange for reaching certain goals helps with motivation. Incentives are fun ways to keep everyone focused on the company and its goals. These incentives don't have to be related to money. They can be fun things

like lunches, massages, prizes, promotions and even trips. Even the smallest incentive can have a big effect.

#73- Learn more about your market.

Constantly expanding your knowledge about your business's market will help fuel new ideas and new concepts. This in turn will keep you motivated to expand your company and to keep up with the modern trends of the business. This will help keep your business always moving in the right direction and will allow you to better your understanding of what your customers want.

#74- There is always tomorrow.

As a Boss Babe there are going to be days when you don't get it right. It is important to remember that there is always tomorrow. Think of tomorrow as a time to get it right and succeed. So if today doesn't go well there is always the chance that tomorrow will be amazing.

#75- Try to have some fun.

Adding a little bit of fun to your everyday life will make your daily tasks more enjoyable and easier to deal with.

#76- Treat the motivation process like a daily task.

Every business has daily and weekly tasks that need to be completed so the business can remain operational. This includes the process of motivating yourself and your workers, so make sure that you treat it as such. Finding ways to stay motivated is essential to keeping your company operational, so make this process part of your everyday tasks.

6

Growing Your Business

If your business isn't growing, then it is failing. If you aren't moving forward, then you are moving backward. Once you have the right people in place and have developed a good customer base your company should focus on continual growth. There are lots of ways to promote growth in your company and the specifics will be based on your particular business.

For example, growth for a retail business may mean opening up a new storefront or developing a new product line. Growth for an IT company could be purchasing or developing a new system. Growth for an author may be publishing 2 books this year instead of 1. Whatever your company does you need to figure out ways to expand it. This goes beyond just figuring out ways to earn more money.

Creating Strong Business Relationships

Creating business relationships that are strong is the foundation of growing your business. Customers, clients, suppliers and business associates are the lifeblood of your business's growth. You simply cannot forge ahead down the path to success without these helpers, which means you need to develop long-lasting and meaningful relationships with them. These relationships are established on trust and honesty.

#77- Communicate often.

Communication between your business contacts is extremely important. This is especially true of your customers and your suppliers. These contacts rely on you to tell them what is going on, which includes letting them in on any problems you are experiencing. Communication should be a top priority for your business relationships.

#78- Meet deadlines.

When a customer deals with your business they expect you to hold up your end of the bargain and deliver on your promises. This certainly means meeting your deadlines. When you promise something to a customer or supplier, you want them to consider your word as your bond. Not having to worry if your business will fulfill its requirements builds trust with customers.

#79- Try to prevent surprises.

Customers and clients generally don't like surprises; especially if the service your company provides has a direct link to their livelihood. While it may not be possible for you to prevent unwanted things from happening, being honest with your customers and maintaining communication with them regarding what is going on can help you to eliminate unwanted surprises.

Being Honest

The value of being an honest business cannot be overstated. Your company will grow faster and reach further if it is based on honest principles and ethics. It is important to strive for honesty at all times and at all levels of your business.

#80- Honesty will keep your customers coming back.

No business relationship can last if it isn't based on honesty. Being honest with your clients and customers will help them want to continue to give you their business. Honesty builds trust and this can create a business reputation that will help you grow and get you more clients.

You should be honest with everyone that has to do with your business, not just your customers and clients. You need to be honest with your employees, your suppliers, your investors and everyone else. This means not making up lies to cover your own basis, owning up to your own mistakes and acknowledging the business's state to your employees and investors. Again, this kind of honesty creates loyalty.

#81- Be honest with yourself.

Don't forget to be honest with yourself too. This can be the most brutal form of honesty and one of the hardest things you can do. Being honest with yourself regarding what you really want from your business and what goals you are really looking to achieve is extremely important. Lying to yourself, even in tiny ways, can end up causing you to compromise your business, its ethics and its principles, which can spell disaster.

#82- Be honest about growth.

Don't try to grow your business too quickly either. There is always the idea that a business a business should grow as quickly as it can, but this concept can often lead to trouble. Sustained business growth comes from a clear and detailed strategy. It also comes from having the appropriate systems and processes ready to go in order to cope with this new growth. Don't focus on everything at one time. Pay attention to the required resources needed to sustain this growth, as many smaller businesses simply don't have access to the right resources and can get in over their heads.

7

Communication Skills

As you already know, communication is vital to both the growth of your business and the ability for your company to sustain its growth. Communication is also important for developing trust with your business associates and with your employees. Good communication skills can help you to motivate employees, drive change, repair conflicts and become a better leader. Listening skills are extremely important for accomplishing these tasks, but there are other communication skills that all Boss Babes need to have.

Better Ways to Communicate

While you are probably pretty good at communicating with other people, there are some better ways to communicate when it comes to running a business. These are evolutionary skills- meaning you develop them over time as a result of your experiences. Learning about some of these skills in advance will help you to incorporate them into your business life sooner.

#83- Good communication skills allow you to influence others.
  The ability to influence others is vital for any Boss Babe. You will

need to sell your employees your business's principles and goals if you want them to get on board. You will have to convince investors and business partners to take a chance and support your business ideas. You will have to influence your customers through marketing and advertising. In order to get your point across and achieve your goal of influencing others you must be able to communicate your ideas well through discussions and offer clear explanations of your thoughts.

#84- Learn how to manage questions well.

As a boss and a leader you will have to answer thousands of questions. Some of these questions will be simple while others will determine the success of your company. It is your job to answer these questions by making convincing arguments using the art of well-versed speaking. Your words must not only answer the question, but they must also convey your meaning, desires and principles at the same time. If you take the time to learn the art, and it is an art, of managing questions well now it will have a positive impact on your career forever.

#85- Holding the audience's attention.

All of the speaking skills in the world won't help you to convey your point if you cannot hold the attention of your audience. Learning how to capture the attention of your listeners is vital, especially in the workplace environment. In order to master this skill you must learn how to read your audience, how to project your voice in a pleasing and attention-getting manner and how to manage your speaking time. If you cannot make people pay attention to you it will be hard to get them to follow you to success.

How to Create Dialog

In addition to using your communication skills to motivate and convince others, you can also use them to capture new ideas, incentives and concepts and use them to your benefit. The best way to accomplish this is to create a dialog. This dialog can be among your managers, employees, peers, customers and even your competitors. Learning how to get a dialog going is another great communication skill that all Boss Babes should have.

#86- Hold face to face interactions.

Getting your employees together for face to face interactions is a great way to get a dialog going and to get the creative juices flowing. Face to face interactions encourages brainstorming and the sharing of ideas in a way that e-mail, text, and telephone conversations simply cannot.

#87- Provide avenues for your employees to communicate.

If you want to encourage dialog between your employees, it is essential that you provide a way for them to do so. You need to give your employees a way to offer their suggestions and ideas.

#88- Make sure you and your management team are approachable.

All of the communication avenues you provide for your employees will be useless if they feel like they cannot approach you or the rest of your management team. Use your communication skills, your actions and your positive attitude to show your employees that they can come to you with their ideas and feedback. Your employees will come to you if you let them.

#89- Act on what you hear.

If your employees see that you are willing to put their ideas and suggestions into action, they will be more likely to share them with you. Also, encouraging a dialog among your workers will help you to develop concepts and ideas you may have never considered before. These breakthrough ideas may never have come to you if you didn't encourage dialog with your employees.

8

Marketing

As a Boss Babe you will have master many skills, including management, communication and decision-making skills. One of the most important aspects that all business owners need to understand is marketing. This will be how you sell your business to its customers and therefore will represent how you will create profits for your business. There is a lot to understand about marketing and plenty of ways to make mistakes. All successful Boss Babes have mastered the art of marketing themselves and their company.

Creating a Marketing Plan

Companies that are successful in marketing themselves start the process by creating a detailed marketing plan. The size and scope of your business's marketing plan will be determined by several factors, including the size of your company and how many potential customers you will attempt to reach. It is a good idea to create your marketing plan and then refer back to it on a monthly basis to ensure that you are still on track. A lot of things can change for a business as the year progresses.

#90- Your business's marketing plan should cover one year of time.

The ideal amount of time to plan ahead for marketing, especially if you run a small business or a start-up business, is one year. There are a lot of things to cover in a year's time. Your business will gain and lose employees, the market will evolve, and your customer base will (hopefully) grow. This represents plenty of time and factors to consider. Once your business develops and grows you can switch to a marketing plan that covers a period of time two to three years in advance.

The process of creating your marketing plan will be the most difficult part. Actually, implementing the plan will be easier than creating it. Expect the process of developing a marketing plan to take several months. The plan should be created using your field of hired experts, including people from your finance, supply, management and personnel departments. Don't forget to hire a marketing expert or experts to help. Make sure to include the input of all your experts to ensure that you are not missing anything.

Your marketing plan will have several benefits for your company, including:

Giving your employees something to rally behind- the marketing plan shows your employees what the company is going to accomplish and how it is going to accomplish these things. This can give every employee a sense of team and purpose to rally behind.

Providing a set of instructions to follow- a marketing plan is just like a set of instructions. It forecasts a step by step plan of how the company plans to succeed, which gives your employees something to follow.

Allowing new employees to jump on board quickly- as your company grows and changes it will take on new employees. The business's marketing plan will clearly define what the company's goals and achievements will be, which will help new employees jump on board and be ready to contribute much faster.

Types of Marketing Campaigns

There are many different types of marketing campaigns and how you decide to market your business will depend heavily on your individual factors. There are several major types of marketing campaigns to consider however, and you may choose to implement several of these campaigns' types simultaneously. Some of the different types of marketing include:

Print advertising- this includes advertising techniques such as magazines, newspapers and flyers. These allow you to get your brand or advertising information out to specific readers and these marketing efforts usually need to be created months in advance.

TV and Radio- television and radio ads can be used to reach an extraordinarily large amount of potential customers at any given time. These are effective yet expensive forms of marketing.

Direct mail- these campaigns focus on brochures, postcards and flyers that are sent to customers through their mail. This technique is rather outdated but still serves some purpose.

Online marketing- online marketing is probably the most cost-effective and most useful type of marketing in today's world. These techniques can encompass websites, email marketing, SEO or organic search engine marketing and social media.

Your marketing team will have to carefully consider a number of factors when it comes up with your business's marketing plan, including your product or service, who you are trying to reach, what message you are trying to send and how much money you are willing to spend to spend on marketing.

#91- Do your marketing research.

Research into your market will be the backbone of how you both create your marketing plan and how you improve upon it. A lack of good market research will cause you to lose potential customers and sales. There are many ways to conduct market research, including but not limited to surveys, focus groups and internet searches.

#92- Determine your target audience ahead of time.

In order to develop an effective way to market to your business's target audience you must know who this audience is first. This will help you find the best ways to reach them. Find out as much about your targeted customers as you can so that you can figure out how to directly reach them in the future.

#93- Clearly define your resources.

You cannot create a detailed marketing plan for your business if you don't know what resources your business has to work with first. Therefore, it is a good idea to clearly define what resources your company has to work with. These resources can include how much money you can devote to marketing, how much staff you can use, and which tactics are available for you.

#94- Make sure your marketing plan is flexible.

Flexibility is an important trait for every business to have, because today's business world is ever changing. This is especially true of your marketing plan. Markets and customers constantly change, and it is vital for your company to be able to change with them. Ensure that your marketing plan takes these changes into account and is always ready to change with the times.

Existing Versus New Customers

One of your most important jobs as a new Boss Babe will be to find new customers through your marketing plan to help your business grow. Once your business is fully developed you will continue this quest. Businesses that are expanding spend a great deal of their time and resources looking for new clients and because of this they will often overlook a very important factor. This factor is the retention of existing clients.

Your current customers are an extremely valuable part of your business. They have helped you attain success so far and are worthy of your loyalty. The fact is that it will cost your business less money to retain its loyal customers than it will to go out and find new customers.

This doesn't mean that you shouldn't be spending resources to generate new clientele, but it does mean that an important part of your marketing plan should be based on keeping the customers you already have. The average company will see annual growth of 3% if they are able to retain all of its existing customers for one more month per year. There are lots of ways to work on retaining your existing customers.

#95– Part of your marketing plan should include customer service.
    One of the best ways to retain your current customers is to make sure they feel appreciated and happy with your business. Customer service and benefits should be included as part of your marketing plan, especially because they cost less than marketing to new clients.

#96– Never assume that your customers will stay.

It is true that most people like to give their business to companies they like and trust. If you provide a good experience to your clients, odds are they will come back the next time. This is a good thing to know, but never assume that your customers will automatically come back to you. There are lots of reasons why a customer may choose to give their business to someone else. Perhaps the other company has lower prices, has opened up a closer storefront or is offering better services. Remember that on average, repeat clients will spend about 33% more money at your business than a new customer will.

#97- Be sincere with your customers.

The relationship you have with your existing customers will go a long way towards determining if they will stay your customers. People are very good at telling when a company is acting insincerely. Consider long-term retention of your existing customers a worthy goal and be very sincere in your efforts. This means nurturing your current relationships and doing your best to make every transaction and interaction as positive as possible.

Online Strategies

Online marketing strategies represent one of the most cost-effective forms of marketing, especially for businesses that are relatively small. There are many forms of online marketing, including e-mail marketing, search engine optimization techniques, social media marketing, lead generation, online branding and straight up online advertising.

While traditional forms of business advertising such as newspaper and television ads are still effective ways to reach potential customers, a vast majority of people will find the businesses they want to use via the internet. This makes online marketing strategies worth their weight in gold.

Online marketing strategies have changed recently. This is because the internet is a constantly changing medium.

If you want to run a successful online marketing campaign you need to be aware of and up to date with these changes. Remember the concept of surrounding yourself with experts. This form of marketing may be one of the best examples of how using the skills of an expert can help your business to succeed. Consider hiring an expert in the world of online marketing.

#98- Always practice white hat marketing techniques.

There are two kinds of online marketing techniques- white hat techniques and black hat tactics. White hat marketing techniques are considered to be honest tactics that rely on hard work to accomplish. Black hat tactics are ways to cheat the system.

These tactics will use systems that steal customer information from others, that blast potential customers with annoying messages, use never-ending link wheels and that load up their website content with keywords in an attempt to generate false search engine results.

Major search engines like Google have ways to find people who use black hat tactics and will punish them severely. Considering how many people use Google to locate companies you should heed this warning. Also, many black hat tactics will alienate and annoy your customers, so it is best to always stick to white hat marketing.

#99- Pay attention to SERPs.

SERPs are search engine results pages. These are the pages that come up when a customer performs a search on major search engines like Google. Research clearly shows that online viewers will only choose companies and websites that are listed on the first SERP page they receive. This means that if your business's website or links leading to its website doesn't appear in the top ten results on a major search engine then people are not finding you.

The desire to achieve high SERP rankings has led to the creation of SEO or search engine optimization. There is an entire world of SEO marketing out there and it is worth your time to ensure that you are optimizing your website for high rankings. SEO can include things like keyword generation, Ad Word campaigns, content marketing, social media use, positive link building and connections with high authority websites. This is another place where an online marketing expert can make a world of difference.

#100- Use social media.

Social media is huge in today's online world. Your customers are using social media, so you should be too. Social media is an inexpensive way to market your company, but it is also extremely useful. For example, you can use various social media platforms to establish your company as an authority in a specific niche, directly connect with customers, create a brand image for your business, resolve customer problems, announce news and updates about your company and improve customer service. All of this can be accomplished extremely cheaply, which makes social media marketing very important.

#101- Use content marketing.

Content marketing is another useful form of online marketing that is both effective and inexpensive. Many companies overlook this form of marketing, which can be a big mistake. Content marketing can include things like podcasts, eBooks, articles, videos, games and blogs. These can be used to inspire confidence and knowledge about your company. In fact, 60% of consumers report having better feelings about companies after they read a custom publication about them. Just make sure that the content you produce is high quality, as low-quality content will make your company look unprofessional in the eyes of your customers and will get you penalized by major search engines such as Google.

9

The Boss Babe's Mindset

There is a significant difference between people who start their own companies and truly successful Boss Babes. Many people start their own businesses, but few people actually achieve the kind of success they dreamed of at the start. What is the difference between people who start up their own business and successful Boss Babes? The answer is the Boss Babe's mindset.

Few people actually think like true Boss Babes. There is a difference between creating a job for yourself and creating a business. A business is something that could still be operational if you, the creator, was to leave. That means that you have been able to create a functional entity, not just a job position where you do all of the work. This is the type of mindset you must have if you want to become a truly successful Boss Babe.

Creating an entrepreneurial mindset starts at the beginning, before you do anything to start up your company. It means having a grand vision and passion. It means carefully considering all that you want your company to be before it even exists. It means imparting your vision, your dreams and your principles into the company right off the bat. You need to ask yourself meaningful questions so that you are able to focus on more than just the day to day functions of running your business.

Your business must be built upon your dreams, your passions and your principles. This is the difference between a job and a business.

In addition to how you view your business, you also need to make sure that your personality and your character are appropriate for the struggles of being a Boss Babe. Becoming a successful Boss Babe is long hard work that takes a lot of dedication. Some of the personality and character traits required to become successful in this venture include organizational skills, the ability to handle pressure, a tolerance for risk, a strong mental drive, a competitive nature, a healthy outlook on life, a positive attitude, decisiveness, patience, optimism and pure strength. This lifestyle also requires self-confidence and independent thought.

It is possible to cultivate a Boss Babe mindset into your daily life if you don't already have one built in. Some people are naturally designed to be amazing Boss Babes, while others have to develop these traits within themselves. It doesn't matter which of these two examples you happen to be. As you have already learned, true entrepreneur-ism comes from passion and desire. If you have the right amount of passion and desire to achieve something, then you will have the appropriate drive to make all necessary changes and alterations to yourself to make these things come true. This is the art of developing a Boss Babe's mindset.

Taking What You Have Learned and Incorporating It into How Yc

Having a Boss Babe's mindset means to incorporate everything that you have learned into how you think and act every single day. It means to focus your energy on what is necessary to succeed in your life, which includes succeeding in your business. The successful Boss Babe does what is necessary to do their job right. This could mean practicing how to focus on the positive aspects, working to overcome your faults and learning as much as you can whenever you can learn it.

A true Boss Babe is never off the clock, even though they know when to work and when to relax. The Boss Babe's mindset can be applied to every aspect of your life, not just to how you run your business. This way of thinking can be used to improve your relationships with your family and friends, how you develop your hobbies and interests and to your parenting skills. Boss Babes are flexible, competent and able learners. There is almost nothing in this life that they cannot do or accomplish, especially if drive and passion is what's behind their motivations.

Living the Boss Babe Lifestyle

There are plenty of benefits to living the Boss Babe lifestyle. For many Boss Babes this lifestyle equals freedom, purpose and enjoyment. It also means hard work and never-ending motivation. The successful Boss Babe lives for their work. This doesn't mean that their job is the only thing in their life- it means that their work is their life's passion. Could you imagine waking up every day to go to a job that you love and cannot wait to do? This is the lifestyle of the successful Boss Babe and is why it is so vitally important for you to choose something that you are truly passionate about.

The Boss Babe's lifestyle is also one of the main reasons why you will want to undergo this amazing transformation. It is why you want to do something different and more meaningful with your life. This is a different choice. It is not the 'rat race' or the 'daily grind'. It is not 'working for the man'. It is working for yourself, by yourself and for what you appreciate the most in life. It is a life choice.

Enjoying Your Success

Hopefully you will have what it takes to become a truly successful Boss Babe and will be able to push yourself to accomplish everything it takes to be successful. If you are able to accomplish these feats, you will be able to experience what few other people in this world will be able to feel- the ability to enjoy your success in life.

Almost all forms of success bring the pleasure and pride of achievement with them, but few will taste as sweet as success that is self-made. It is truly an amazing thing to be able to look at your successful life, which includes your passion, your dream, your ability to live the kind of life you want and your financial security and know that it was you who achieved it! So, few people have only themselves to thank for the amazing life they live. This feeling is worth more than any money or material possessions you can think of. It is a feeling that can only be experienced through the success of entrepreneurship.

The purpose behind becoming a Boss Babe is to take the time to truly stop and enjoy your success. If not, what is the point of all of your hard work?

So, if you think you have what it takes to take on the challenge and develop an entrepreneurial mindset, you should immediately begin the process of doing so. The good news is that there are numerous tools available to help you along the way. From mastering the basic skills and personality traits of successful business owners to learning the finer points of marketing a company, there are hundreds of thousands of learning tools out there to help you achieve your goals. If you are willing to learn the knowledge it will be easily presented to you.

The best advice anyone can give an aspiring Boss Babe is to take advantage of the informational world we live in and to learn as much as you can whenever you can. Smart people take every advantage they can find, and the vast amounts of knowledge available is certainly a considerable advantage. Learn what you need to know to become a successful Boss Babe and then create a mindset within yourself that allows you to make the appropriate changes to your physical and mental self. There is nothing you cannot do if you set your mind to it!

AUTHOR * PODCASTER * VLOGGER

About the Author

Abiegail Rose is a writer, singer, and motivator. She loves filling in the black and white lines of life with dramatic colors, and she is always ready to interact with her readers and listeners.

You can connect with me on:

🌐 http://www.BossBabePublications.com

📘 http://facebook.com/BossBabePublications

🔗 http://instagram.com/BossBabybyDesign

Also by Abiegail Rose

The Carter Effect

In her debut non-fiction book, Abiegail shows you how to harness your experiences and turn them into passion and profit.

Listening to Beyoncé and Jay Z helped her to zone into the roadmap that leads to becoming a person of influence, impact, and inspiration.

You have incredible untapped potential residing within yourself in your own talents and abilities, it's hiding right underneath the pain and doubt.

This book shows you how to achieve all your goals by putting a focus on the lyrical and business geniuses that are Beyoncé and Jay-Z.